Abracadabra Piano

Book 2

Graded pieces for the young pianist

Selected and arranged by Jane Sebba

Consultant – Sonia Harris

Illustrations – Gunvor Edwards

A & C Black • London

For the children who have tried and tested the pieces in this book, especially Oliver, William and Tom.

First published 1993
by A & C Black (Publishers) Ltd
35 Bedford Row, London WC1R 4JH

© 1993 Jane Sebba
Text illustrations © Gunvor Edwards
Cover illustration © Cathie Felstead
Edited by Sheena Roberts
Type and music set by Figaro
Printed in Great Britain
by St Edmundsbury Press

ISBN 0-7136-3725-0

To your teacher

Abracadabra Piano is a repertoire book intended to be used alongside your usual piano tutor. But besides the learning of a wide range of repertoire pieces there are many other things to be gained from using this book. With Abracadabra Piano, beginners of all ages can

* *play immediately without written music*
* *enjoy scales and fingering exercises*
* *improvise and compose*
* *develop a range of aural skills*

In fact all the games in this book are designed to build confidence from the very beginning of piano playing, and to counter before they have a chance to set in, the self-consciousness and panic which inhibit musical freedom. Try the games, the improvising, the composing with pupils of all ages, at all stages, and especially with beginners. They will be luckier than those of us who were glued to the written music and helpless without it.

Of course, being able to read music is extremely important, but not exclusively so. Pupils must learn to read music but they must also develop an ear. The many suggestions throughout the book which encourage this will broaden your pupils' musical experience and develop skills they will need for aural tests, theory and GCSE exams in years to come. They will also be covering many areas of National Curriculum Music.

From the earliest stages, beginners can be given opportunities for improvising, transposing, imitating and playing without written music. Even if you are not a natural improviser yourself, and don't play very much by ear, try not to confine your pupils' skills to playing only from music. We don't expect them to read a foreign language without first hearing the sounds of the words. Let us not expect our musical beginners to read music and know how to produce the sounds without first hearing them. Learning by imitation works! and success fuels enthusiasm and progress – so vitally important to the beginner.

Some technical points

* *Every encounter with music should start with a moment's thought about the tempo. Pupils should be able to count themselves in. Pianists often play on their own and don't learn the good habits of establishing a pulse and keeping a tempo.*

* *Don't always sit your pupil opposite middle C. Many pieces in this book require that they are based elsewhere.*

* *Use activities such as* Finish the melody, Your turn my turn, Cat and mouse *and* Be an inventor *frequently and whenever you like, not just when you get to the relevant page. The more practice the better.*

* *Sometimes, a break from the keyboard can benefit everyone. Try learning new rhythms by clapping hands, tapping knees, clicking fingers, etc. A song like* Clap your hands and wiggle your fingers *(Book 1) is good for loosening up mind and body, and children may well have encountered activities like this at school.*

* *Some pieces are intended to be taught by rote. (Look at the music together later; a very important stage.) Learning by rote is a skill in its own right; help your pupils to develop it.*

* *Because many young beginners can't reach the pedals, pedalling has not been included in the book as a teaching point. If your pupils' legs are long enough do use pedalling where appropriate.*

* *Show your pupils how to make a piece of music their own: include the names of people they know, their school, their address, pet, etc. When you do this, your pupil may need to change rhythms and notation to fit the new words or syllables. That's good. It will encourage freedom, initiative and improvisation.*

Above all, Abracadabra Piano aims to encourage enjoyment and fun at the keyboard. It will set up your pupils (children and adults) to succeed, and will make their musical ladder easier to climb. They will take the listening skills they learn at the piano into many areas of life.

Jane Sebba, London 1993

Contents

Early in the morning

traditional, arr. JS

Here is a song to sing and play, and then you can change it to make it your own.

Here's what you can change.

Change the name each time. Instead of *Imogen* put in your own and your friends' names. Change the rhythm to fit.

Ma-de-leine

A - le-xan-der

Change the person who knocks and what they bring.

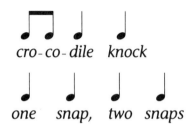

cro-co-dile knock

one snap, two snaps

To your teacher
The tune works as a round with entries at two-bar intervals. Two or more pupils can play it in different octaves.

4

Quietly – don't wake anyone

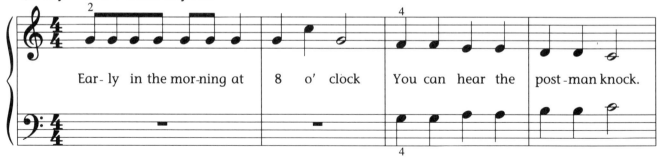

Ear- ly in the mor-ning at 8 o' clock You can hear the post-man knock.

Louder – it's time they got up

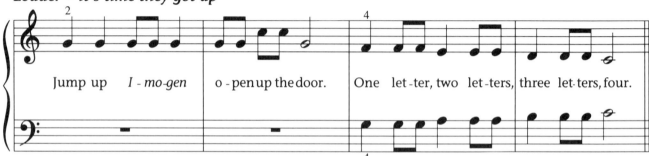

Jump up I - mo-gen o - pen up the door. One let-ter, two let-ters, three let-ters, four.

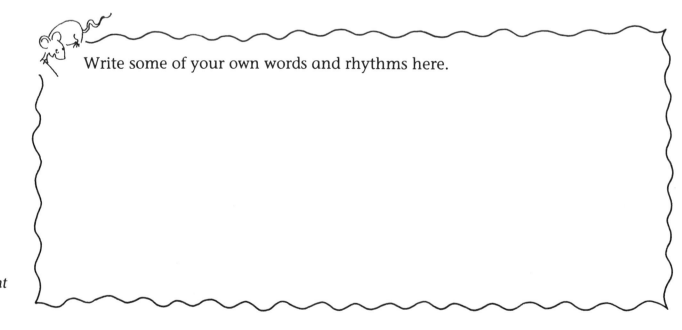

Write some of your own words and rhythms here.

Green grow the rushes-oh

traditional, arr. JS

Firmly

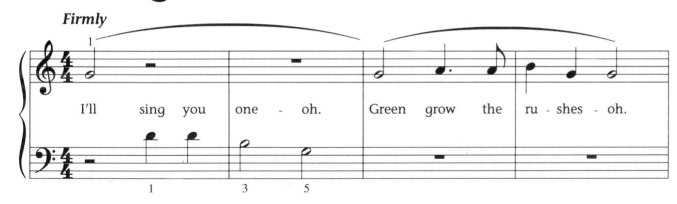

I'll sing you one - oh. Green grow the ru - shes - oh.

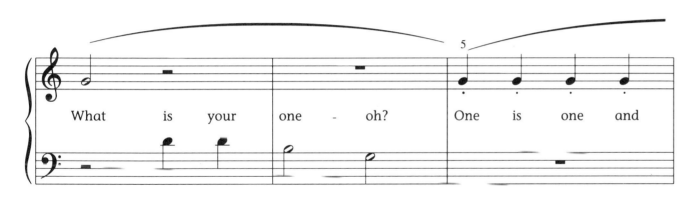

What is your one - oh? One is one and

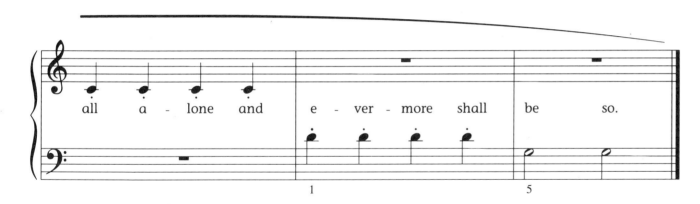

all a - lone and e - ver - more shall be so.

☆ After you have learnt this piece, start it on a different note. Try C or D.

To your teacher
It may be helpful to play alternate phrases with your pupil while learning the piece.

5

Cat and mouse

Here are three cat and mouse tunes – they sound just like a cat stalking a mouse. Wherever the mouse goes, the cat follows.

Play them with your teacher like this. You are the cat, so be a clever copycat and follow the mouse wherever it goes. Listen out for staccato notes, or loud parts, or anything else your mouse may do, and copy it exactly.

To your teacher
You may like to start by clapping the rhythms of the tunes.

6

Old MacDonald had a piano

traditional, arr. JS

Be ready to play C on old MacDonald's piano. You can play any C, anywhere on the keyboard.

Think of something else to play on Old MacDonald's piano.
Instead of C, you could play:

octaves   **chords**

F#

rests

quavers

loud sounds

high sounds

Old Mac-Do - nald had a pia - no, Ee - i - ee - i - o.

On that pia-no he had some Cs Ee - i - ee - i - o. (With a)

C C here (and a) C C there, Here a C, there a C, ev'-ry-where a C C

Old Mac-Do - nald had a pia - no, Ee - i - ee - i - o.

For your teacher

Your turn, my turn

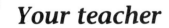

Choose a song you know well. Sing it with your teacher, then clap the words as you sing it again. Now take turns, like this.

Your teacher	You
* * * * * * *	* * * * * * *
Lon-don Bridge is fall-ing down,	**fall-ing down, fall-ing down,**
* * * * * * *	* * * *
Lon-don Bridge is fall-ing down,	**my Fair La-dy.**
* * * * * * *	* * * * * * *
Twin-kle, twin-kle, lit-tle bat,	**How I won-der what you're at.**
* * * * * * *	* * * * * * *
Up a-bove the world you fly,	**Like a tea-tray in the sky,**
* * * * * * *	* * * * * * *
Twin-kle, twin-kle, lit-tle bat,	**How I won-der what you're at.**
* * * * * * *	* * * * * *
Lost a mar-ble, lost a mar-ble,	**Lost a mar-ble in the rain,**
* * * * * * *	* * * * * * *
Now it's lost and gone for-e-ver,	**Saw it va-nish down the drain.**

Make sure you keep the song going at a steady speed. If you hesitate or jump in too quickly you lose a point (and the same goes for your teacher).

See who loses more points.

☀ Swap with your teacher so that you start the song.

✹ Sing the words silently in your head while you clap out loud.

✳ Instead of clapping, tap your knees, or click your fingers.

Now learn to play the songs. When you know them well enough, take turns with your teacher again.

It's still just as important not to hesitate or play too quickly – keep the pulse going.

27/9/00
By ♡

London Bridge

22/9/00
Go as far as you want

Lon - don Bridge is fall - ing down, fall - ing down, fall - ing down,

Lon - don Bridge is fall - ing down, my Fair La - dy.

Twinkle, twinkle

Fine

Twin - kle, twin - kle, lit - tle bat, How I won - der what you're at.

D.C. al fine

Up a - bove the world you fly, Like a tea - tray in the sky,

Lost a marble

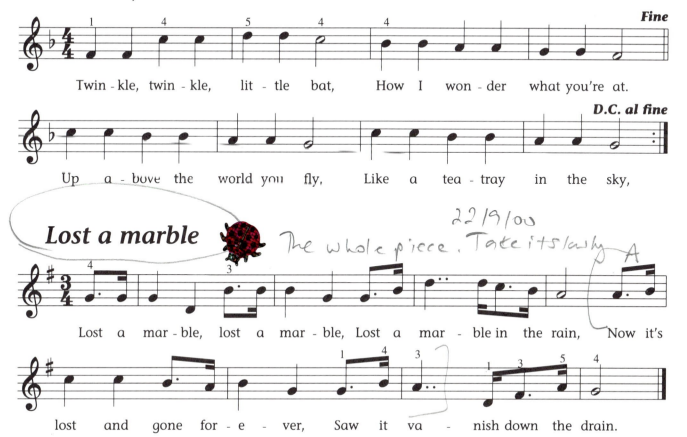

22/9/00
The whole piece. Take it slowly

Lost a mar - ble, lost a mar - ble, Lost a mar - ble in the rain, Now it's

lost and gone for - e - ver, Saw it va - nish down the drain.

To your teacher
This is an exercise in maintaining a steady pulse when singing, then playing.

9

Accents

An accent looks like this >

When you accent a note in music, you lean on it, making it sound louder. We accent words all the time when we are speaking because accents change the meaning of what we say.

Try saying this sentence six times. Each time, put an accent on a different word and listen to how it changes what you mean.

Hàve you seen our black cat?

Have **yòu** seen our black cat?

Have you **sèen** our black cat?

Have you seen **òur** black cat?

Have you seen our **blàck** cat?

Have you seen our black **càt**?

Now try playing some music with this sentence. Play it six times and each time put an accent on a different note.

Lean on the note to accent it, but don't try to push the piano through the floor!

Have   you   seen   our   black   cat?

Make up your own music to fit the words, then write it down here.

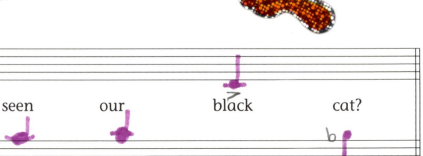

Have   you   seen   our   black   cat?

Draw an accent on a piece of paper. You can trace this one.

Stick a blob of Blu-tack to the back, then you can put your accent over any note in your tune. Move your accent around and listen to the way the music changes.

10

Black key busker

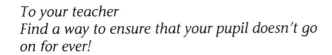

Here is a piece of music for your teacher to play. Your job is to make up some music to go with it. You are going to improvise.

Improvising means making up music in your head, then whooshing it down your arms, through your fingers and on to the keyboard without even stopping for tea. Because it's *your* music, whatever you play will be right, so no one can grumble at you for playing wrong notes.

In this piece there are just two rules:

1 You can *only* play on the black keys.

2 You have to decide when and how to stop, and give your teacher an advance warning (like slowing down, or getting softer, or some other signal) so that you can stop together.

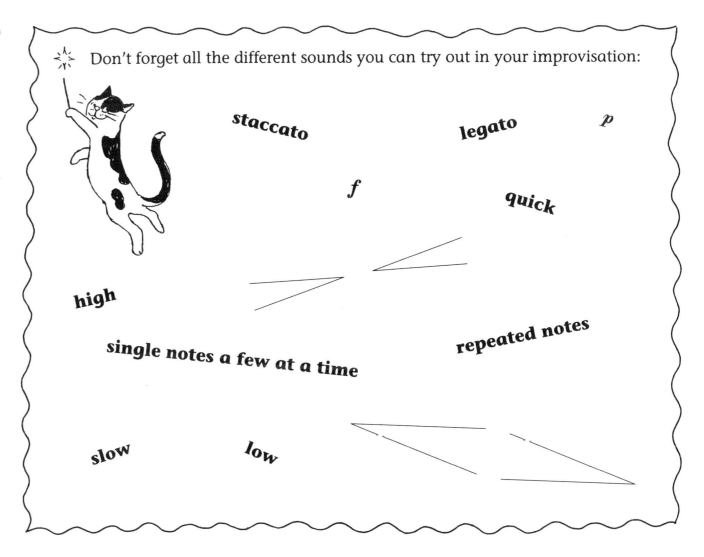

Don't forget all the different sounds you can try out in your improvisation:

staccato   legato   *p*

f   quick

high

single notes a few at a time   repeated notes

slow   low

To your teacher
Find a way to ensure that your pupil doesn't go on for ever!

For your teacher

repeat as necessary

Kookaburra

traditional Australian, arr. JS

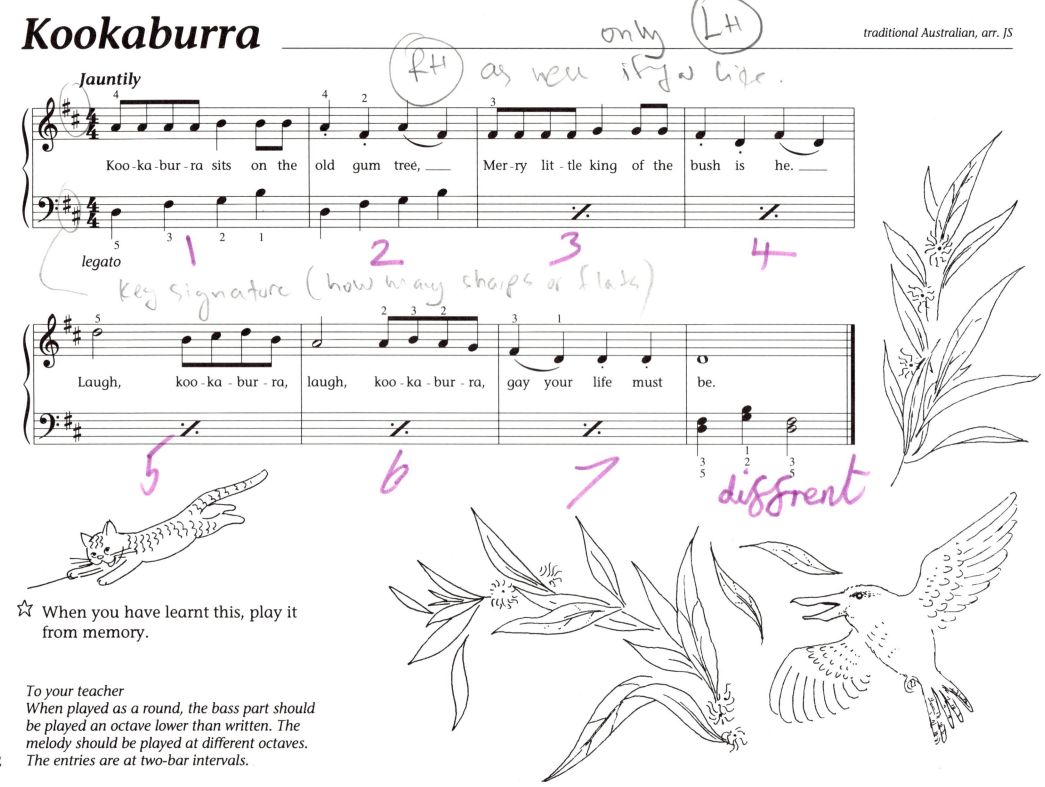

Jauntily

Koo-ka-bur-ra sits on the old gum tree, ___ Mer-ry lit-tle king of the bush is he. ___

legato

Laugh, koo-ka-bur-ra, laugh, koo-ka-bur-ra, gay your life must be.

only (LH)
(RH) as well if you like.

1 2 3 4

key signature (how many sharps or flats)

5 6 7 different

☆ When you have learnt this, play it from memory.

To your teacher
When played as a round, the bass part should be played an octave lower than written. The melody should be played at different octaves. The entries are at two-bar intervals.

12

Miaou, miaou

Jacqueline Mani

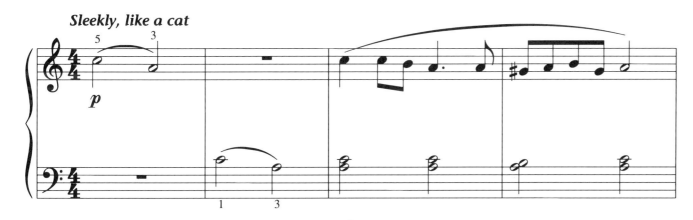

Which notes in this piece sound like a cat miaouing?

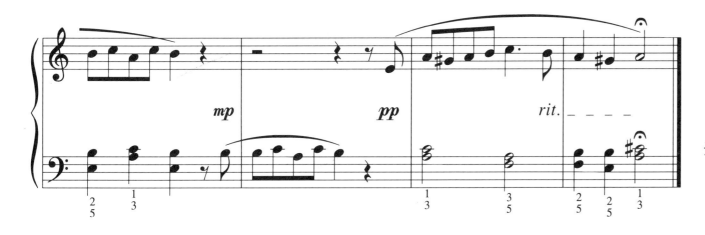

✳ Can you play some cat music of your own? Your cat can be in any mood. Can your teacher guess which?

13

Heart and soul

Heart and soul was written by the jazz musician, Hoagy Carmichael. Do you know this version of it?

20/10/00

After 1/2 Term

Play this piece in different ways. Here's how.

Top part

✳ Play an octave higher.

☆ Play with both hands an octave apart.

☼ Start loud and get quieter throughout.

✸ Start quiet and get louder throughout.

✤ Play staccato.

✩ Play legato.

✴ Think of something yourself.

Bass part

✳ Change the rhythm to this

pink e - le-phant, pink e - le-phant

☼ Play a chord in the **RH**

☆ Play three chords in the **RH**

✳ Start loud and get quieter (with the top part).

☆ Start quiet and get louder (while your partner does the opposite).

✩ Think of something yourself.

Changing from major to minor

Play this scale of C major with your right hand and sing the numbers as you go.
(Use the correct scale fingering.)

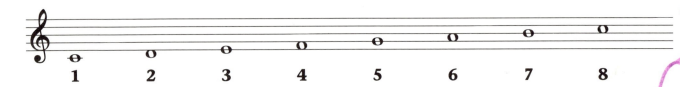

1   2   3   4   5   6   7   8

Now play this.

1   2   3   4   5   6   7   8

By flattening notes 3 and 6 you have
changed the scale of C major into
C minor.

✴ In the same way change some more
scales from major to minor.

Ask your teacher to play the piece
by Mahler on the next page.

It is written in the key of D minor.

Now ask your teacher to play it
again in D major. Do you recognise
it? Which version do you prefer? Do
you like them both?

Ask your teacher to play *Baa baa
black sheep* or another tune you like
in a minor key. Then you can try
playing it too.

Melody from Mahler's First Symphony

Gustav Mahler

20/10/00

A composer named Mahler wrote a symphony and gave this melody to the double bass.

Seriously

While your **LH** plays the melody your **RH** can play these notes eight times over as an accompaniment.

This is called an ostinato – the same snippet of music played over and over again. An ostinato can be a melody, a pattern of chords, or even just a rhythm.

After you have played this as it is written, start it on a different note and transpose it. Try starting on A. Remember to change the ostinato as well.

17

Finish the melody

These melodies come in two sections: a question and an answer. Only the question is given each time. You need to make up an answer using the notes in the answer box.

Whatever you make up will be right, because you are the only person who knows what you want. You can play the notes in any order, in any octave, one at a time or together – whatever you feel makes a good answer to the question.

- Make up several different answers for these questions.

- Ask your teacher to give you some new questions.

- Make up some questions for your teacher to answer.

18

Hineh ma tov

traditional Israeli, arr. JS

With a gentle swing

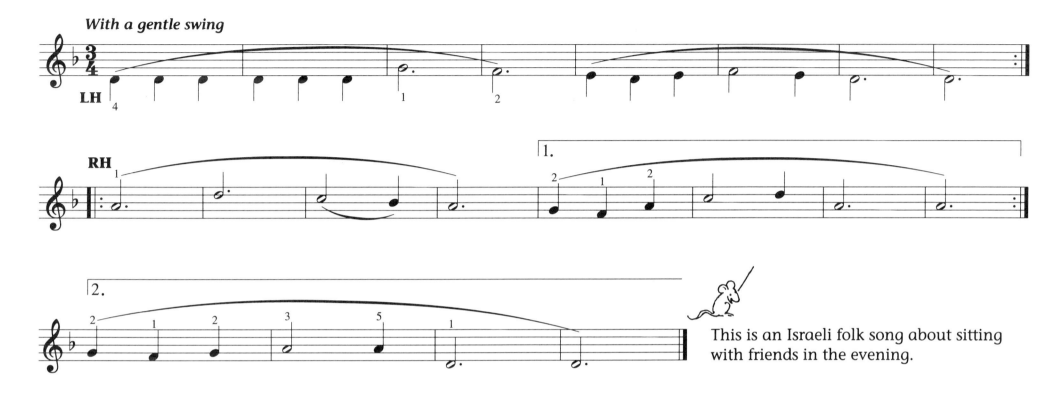

This is an Israeli folk song about sitting with friends in the evening.

For your teacher

To your teacher
This works as a two-part round. The second player begins as the first starts the second line of music. Play the melody an octave higher than written if necessary.

If performed as a round, play only the first eight bars of the accompaniment and repeat them as many times as you need to.

19

An Dro I and II

Breton dance tunes arr. JS

With a steady dance beat

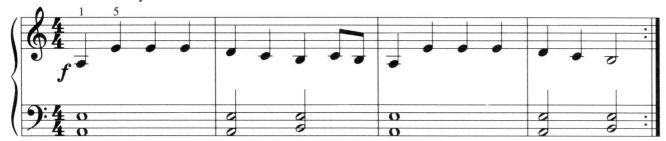

An Dro is the name of a folk dance from Brittany in France and these are two tunes played while people dance the *An Dro*.

When you know both tunes, run them together to make one longer tune.

first time only

second time

Play the **LH** part while you sing the tune.

20

Drums and fyfe

Wilfred Burns, arr. JS

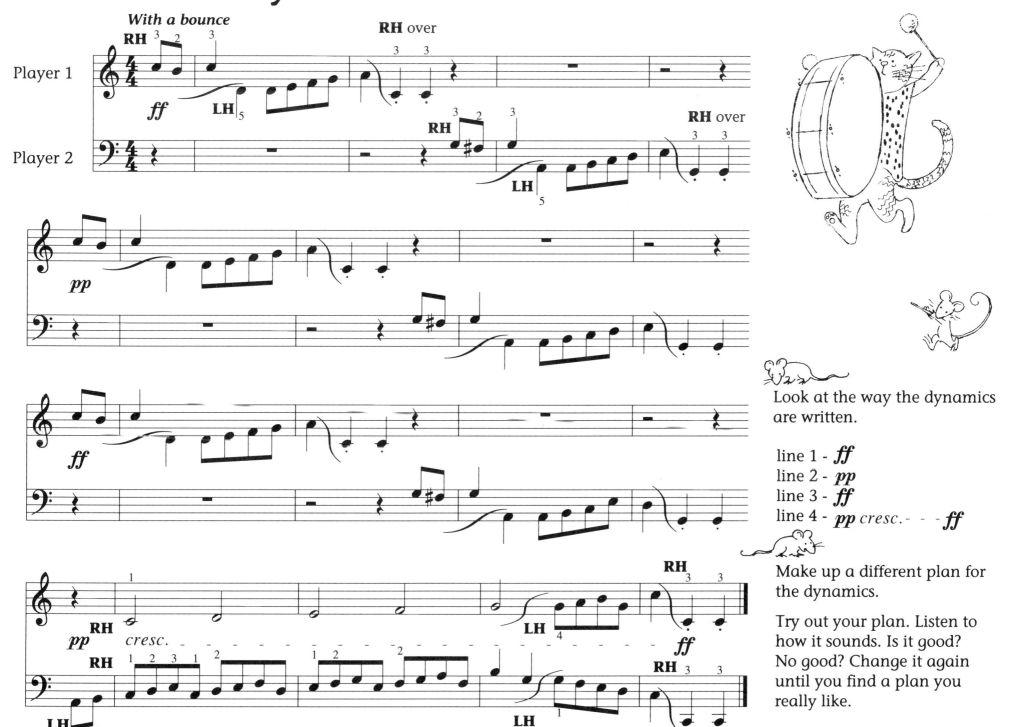

Look at the way the dynamics are written.

line 1 - *ff*
line 2 - *pp*
line 3 - *ff*
line 4 - *pp cresc.* - - - *ff*

Make up a different plan for the dynamics.

Try out your plan. Listen to how it sounds. Is it good? No good? Change it again until you find a plan you really like.

Crossover

traditional North American, arr. JS

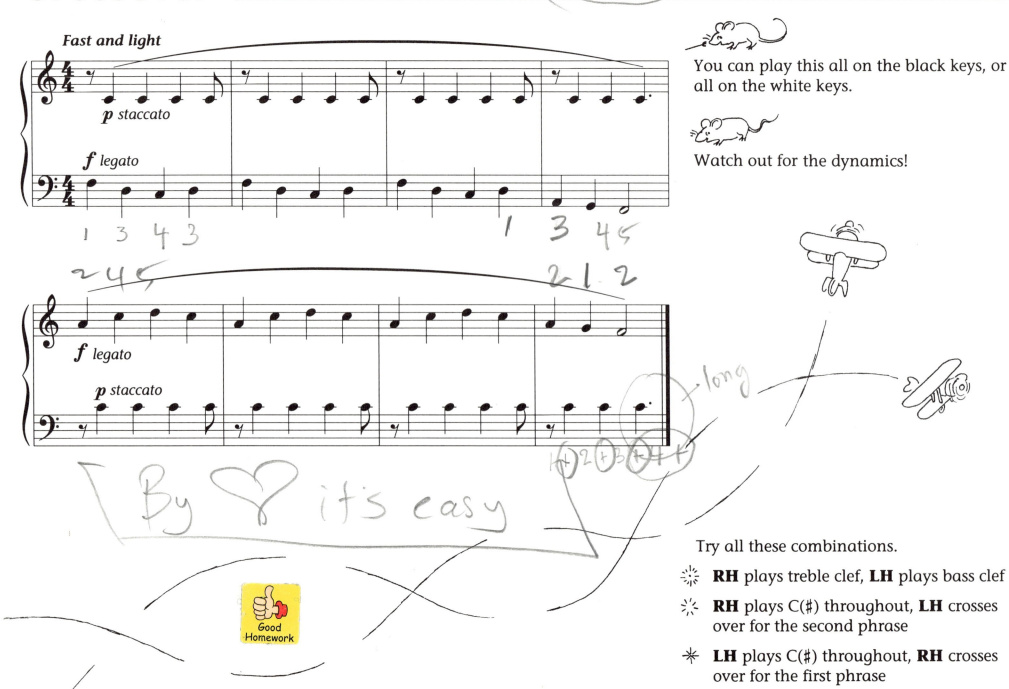

Fast and light

p staccato

f legato

You can play this all on the black keys, or all on the white keys.

Watch out for the dynamics!

f legato

p staccato

[By ♥ it's easy]

Good Homework

Try all these combinations.

- **RH** plays treble clef, **LH** plays bass clef
- **RH** plays C(♯) throughout, **LH** crosses over for the second phrase
- **LH** plays C(♯) throughout, **RH** crosses over for the first phrase
- **RH** plays bass clef, **LH** plays treble clef

Jenny pluck pears

traditional, arr. JS

Be an inventor

Try playing the scale of C major in your **LH** and say **ready** *steady go* to fit the notes. Your teacher will show you how.

Now try fitting the notes to these words:

Jump *in the deep end*

Swim *across the pool*

Very *nearly there*

We *are the winners*

☆ Play a different scale while you say the words.
☆ Start at the bottom and go up.
✳ Put on your inventor's hat and make up some rhythms of your own. Use the names of places you know, book titles, television programmes – anything you like.

To your teacher
*The suggested scale can be played with the **LH** as written, then with **RH** instead, starting with thumb.*

24

Heigh-ho

words by Larry Morey, music by Frank Churchill, arr. JS

Seven-dwarfs-marching tempo

'Heigh - ho, heigh - ho,' to make your troub - les go, just keep on sing - ing

all day long 'Heigh - ho, heigh - ho, heigh - ho, heigh - ho, heigh - ho,' for

it you're feel - ing low, you po - si - tive - ly can't go wrong with a 'Heigh, heigh - ho.'

For your teacher (optional accompaniment)
Jazzily à la walking bass

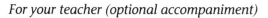

pupil's part starts here

25

German tune

traditional, arr. JS

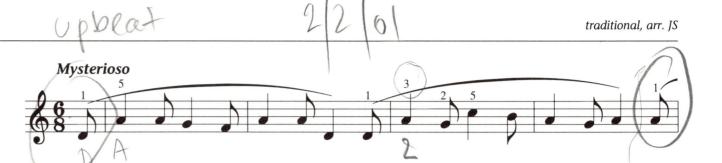

Some music isn't in a major or a minor key. This melody is written in a *mode*. Do you like it?

Your **LH** can play an ostinato accompaniment, while your **RH** plays the melody.

The ostinato in this piece is a pattern of chords. The notes of the chords are D + A, D + G, then D + A again. Look at this music to see some of the different ways you can play the chords.

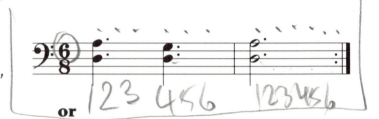

Try all these and decide which you prefer, then accompany the melody with the one you have chosen.

or

How many times do you play the ostinato if you begin and end at the same time as the melody?

or

or

26

Catch a canon

This piece of music is a canon. Can you work out what is special about a canon? Here's a clue. Play the **RH** part on its own, then play the **LH** part. What do you notice?

Another name for a canon is a *catch*. Why do you think this is?

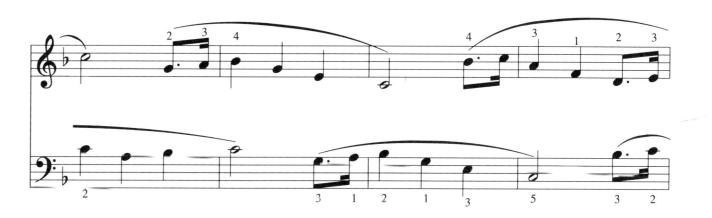

☀ Play the piece as a duet with your teacher.
☀ Swap parts.
☀ Start the bass part before the treble. Which do you prefer?

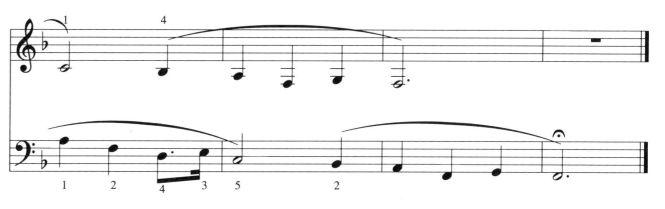

Nonesuch

traditional, arr. JS

This is a lively pop song from around the year 1650. How old is it? In those days people danced to pop songs just as they do now so play it with a good rhythmic beat.

When you know the piece, make it sound different by
- playing the **RH** an octave higher
- playing the **LH** chord in this rhythm

Make up a dynamic plan – it needn't be the same each time you play the piece.

How many beats are there in the last bar? Do you know why?

28

Design-a-piece

1

2

3

4

Music can be written down in different ways. These are some pieces of music which have been written down as pictures. See if you can sing them, then play them. There is no right or wrong way – just sing and play what you think the pictures say.

✧ Turn the book upside down and sing and play the pictures that way up.

✳ Draw some music pictures of your own – you can use any shapes or signs that seem right for your piece of music. This is *your* composition so have fun with it.

☆ Give one of your pictures to someone else to play.

Count-ability

Counting is very important in music.

Many tunes fit to a count of 2, or 3, or 4. You can make up words that go well with these different counts. Try saying and clapping these a few times.

1	2
Left	**right**

1	2	3
Su -	**per** -	**man**

1	2	3	4
Fee	**fi**	**fo**	**fum**

You can make up phrases for other counts too. Here are some more counts to say and clap.

1	2	3	4	5
What's	**on**	**the**	**T**	**V?**

1	2	3	4	5	6
Bi -	**cy** -	**cle**	**tri** -	**cy** -	**cle**

1	2	3	4	5	6	7
Ab -	**ra** -	**ca** -	**dab** -	**ra**	**Pia** -	**no**

30

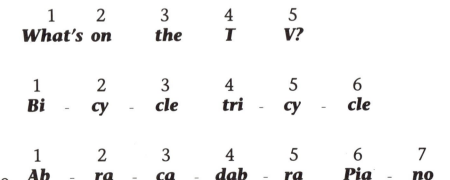

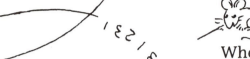

When you can say and clap the counts really well, make up some music to go with them. There are some ideas given here, but you can make up your own – and your own words too.

Before you play these, get the count going by counting a bar to yourself. Whisper –

1 2 or 1 2 3 or whatever.

Left right   Su-per-man

Fee   fi   fo   fum

What's   on   the   T   V?

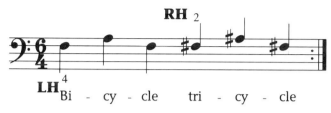

Bi - cy - cle tri - cy - cle

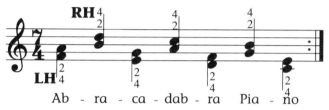

Ab - ra - ca - dab - ra Pia - no

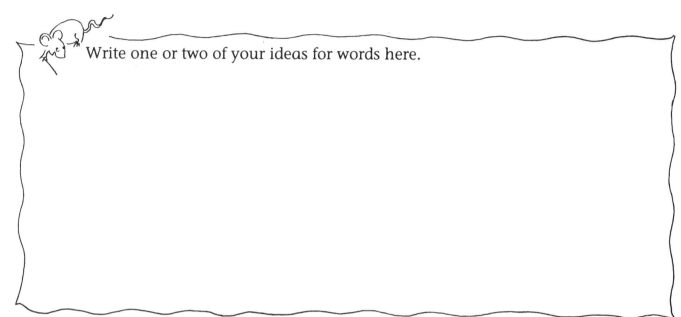

Write one or two of your ideas for words here.

To your teacher
Your pupil might enjoy a pattern of actions to
help emphasise the strong beats, e.g.

tap			tap	
knees	clap	clap	knees	clap
1	2	3	4	5
What's	on	the	T	V?

When Hard Fact is played as a round only one
*person should play the **LH** part which can*
*be transposed down an octave. The **RH***
entries are at one-bar intervals and should be
played in different octaves.

Hard fact

Jan Holdstock

Seven-legged marching tempo

1 - 2 - 3 - 4 - 5 - 6 - 7   All good child - ren go to heav'n

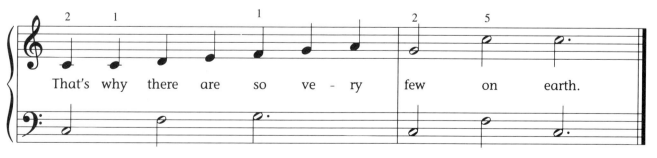

That's why there are so ve - ry   few on earth.

Player 1

Player 2

Ask your teacher to show you how to play this duet. Don't read the music yet.

When you can play it, look at the patterns made by the notes in the written music, and on the keyboard.

✢ Ask someone to sing the melody (Player 1) while you play the accompaniment (Player 2).

✻ Play the accompaniment and sing the melody yourself.

32

☆ Think about different ways to play this piece, e.g.
- dreamy and floating
- heavy and plodding like elephants

❁ Think of some other ways. When you have decided on one you like, make up a suitable title and write it in the space at the top of the page.

My bonny lies over the ocean

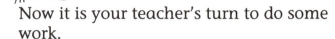

traditional, arr. JS

Gently swaying (but not seasickly)

My bon-ny lies o-ver the o-cean, __ My bon-ny lies o-ver the sea. My

bon-ny lies o-ver the o-cean, __ Oh bring back my bon-ny to me.

Bring back, bring back, oh bring back my bon-ny to me, to me.

Bring back, bring back, oh bring back my bon-ny to me.

Ostinato accompaniments

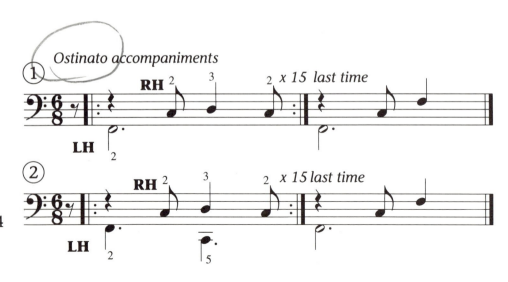

Now it is your teacher's turn to do some work.

Ask your teacher to play

the first ostinato while you both sing the song

the melody while you play the first ostinato

the second ostinato while you both sing the song

the melody while you play the second ostinato

either ostinato while you play and sing the melody

in the key of F# major while you play the tune starting on C#

How well did your teacher do?

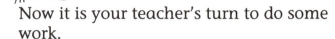

34

Blow wind blow

traditional Gujerati, arr. JS

Lilting

Blow, ___ wind, ___ blow. blow, ___ wind, ___ blow.

Dance with my leaves as you blow, ___ wind, ___ blow.

35

Favourites

Say and play these questions and answers with your teacher.

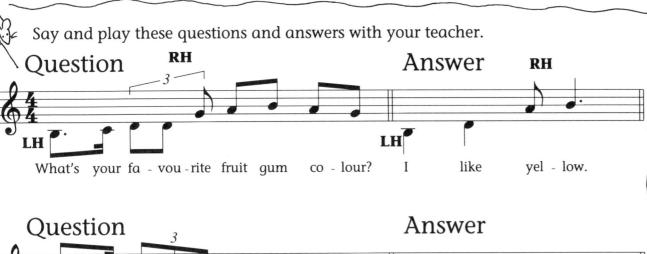

Question — RH — Answer — RH

LH

What's your fa-vou-rite fruit gum co-lour? I like yel-low.

Question — Answer

Where's your fa-vou-rite ho-li-day place? It's the sea-side.

Question — Answer

Who's your fa-vou-rite tea-cher? Mis - sis Jones.

✧ Make up your own tunes for the answers using these notes.

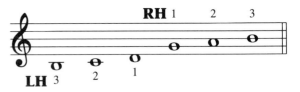

RH 1 2 3

LH 3 2 1

☀ Make up your own answers as well as your own tunes.

☆ Make up some questions to say and play for your teacher.

☀ Write one or two of your questions and answers here.

Optional accompaniment

To your teacher
First say these questions and answers with your pupil in a clear rhythm and with a steady beat. Then sing them. Then while you are singing, clap, or tap your knees, or tap your shoulders.

When your pupil can do all this confidently, introduce the notes.

On the river banks

traditional Hungarian, arr. JS

This beautiful melody swaps from hand to hand. Can you imagine looking from one river bank across to the opposite one?

Add your own dynamics.

Migaldi Magaldi

traditional, arr. JS

Jaunty but not too fast

To your teacher
It may be helpful for your pupil to learn the bass
part of this duet first. (Yes, it really is a B♮ in bars 6 and 8!)

Not enough Air on a G string

words by Jonathan Dove and JS, music by J.S. Bach

The melody is quite hard to play so leave it for your teacher. Use both hands to play your part and be a musical detective: work out what makes it easy.

When you know it well, try playing the bass part and singing the tune at the same time. You will need to take big breaths.

1 2 3 O'Leary

traditional, arr. JS

This rhyme is for bouncing a ball against a wall. After you have learnt it, your **RH** can be lazy and stay where it is. Your **LH** can go off on an adventure and play the tune in any octave you can reach. Cross your **LH** over your **RH** if necessary.

Lively

1 2 3 O' Lea-ry, 4 5 6 O' Lea-ry, 7 8 9 O' Lea-ry, 10 O' Lea-ry Post-man.

Sitting alone

JS

With a gentle swing

Memorise both these pieces, then play them without the music.

Lament

John York

Here is a challenge.

After you have learnt the notes, look at
all the musical directions.

When you play the piece again, try to do
exactly as the directions say and get
every detail correct.

Britches full of stitches

traditional Irish, arr. JS

These two Irish tunes are for dancing the polka so be sure to play them with a swing.

When you know both these polkas, play them one after the other without a gap in between. That's how Irish fiddlers play dance tunes.

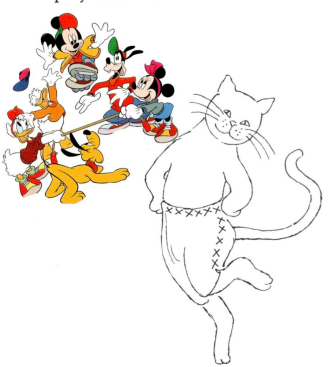

To your teacher
*While learning the **RH**, your pupil can accompany it with a simple **LH** ostinato:*

Britches   Egan's polka

42

Egan's polka

8/2/02

traditional Irish, arr. JS

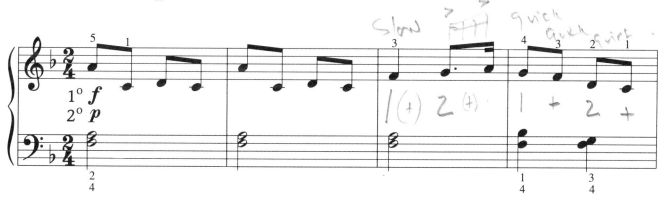

The **LH** chords in *Britches* make a pattern.

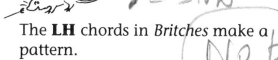

Draw a pattern for the **LH** chords in *Egan's polka*.

Choosing chords for songs you know

Some songs can be accompanied using just two chords: chord I and chord V.

This is how to build the chords so you can play them while you sing.

Chord I

With your **LH**, play the first five notes of the C major scale. Sing the numbers as you play.

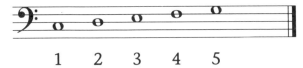

1   2   3   4   5

Now play notes 1, 3 and 5 all together. This is the chord of C major.

 Write the chord here.

Chord V

Build the same pattern (1, 3 and 5) starting on note 5 of C major. This is the chord of G major.

 Write the chord here.

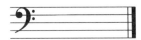

Play chord I (C E G) and chord V (G B D) a few times to get used to them.

44

Using chords I and V

Sing these two songs, and accompany yourself with chords I and V. Decide which chord sounds best where you see ∗.

Listen carefully to hear the difference.

To your teacher
Use I and V in any key – don't get stuck in C. Encourage your pupil to accompany other songs they know well, e.g. London Bridge, The mulberry bush, Sur le pont d'Avignon, Rabbit ain't got no tail.

One man went to mow (Start singing the tune on E)

  ∗   ∗   ∗   ∗

One man went to mow,   went to mow a meadow

  ∗   ∗   ∗   ∗

One man and his dog,   went to mow a meadow.

There's a brown girl in the ring (Start singing the tune on C)

      ∗   ∗

There's a brown girl in the ring tra la la la la,

      ∗   ∗

There's a brown girl in the ring tra la la la la la,

  ∗   ∗

Brown girl in the ring tra la la la la,

  ∗   ∗   ∗   ∗

For she like su-gar and I like plum.

Muck!

traditional, arr. JS

This is a three-part round which uses the chords you have just learned to build.

When you have played it in C, change to another key.

To your teacher
*Ask your pupil to sing the song; then sing and add the **LH** chords; finally play the melody and **LH** chords together.*

The round entries are at eight-bar intervals.

Oh you can't put your muck in our dust-bin, our dust-bin, our dust-bin, you
etc.

I   I   V   I

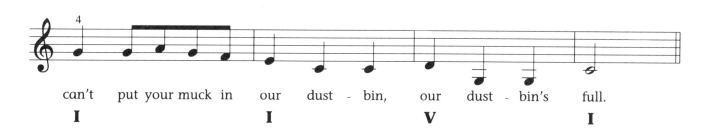

can't put your muck in our dust-bin, our dust-bin's full.

I   I   V   I

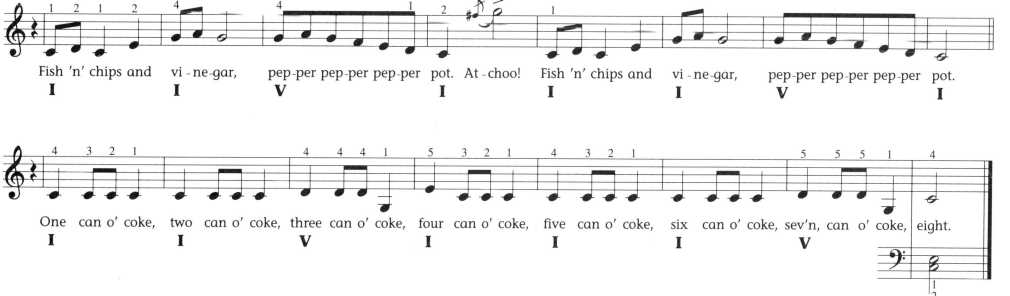

Fish 'n' chips and vi-ne-gar, pep-per pep-per pep-per pot. At-choo! Fish 'n' chips and vi-ne-gar, pep-per pep-per pep-per pot.

I   I   V   I   I   I   V   I

One can o' coke, two can o' coke, three can o' coke, four can o' coke, five can o' coke, six can o' coke, sev'n, can o' coke, eight.

I   I   V   I   I   I   V   I

45

Doll's funeral

P.I. Tchaikovsky

This is the beginning of a piece of music written by Tchaikovsky for young pianists.

Una corda =
one string =
Sounds softer